THE MUSIC INDUSTRY BIBLE

How 2 Not Get Screwed

10 MUSIC INDUSTRY COMMANDMENTS

CHRIS REESE

CONTENTS

DEDICATION

All of this would not be possible without my Family, my Friends, Haters and my crazy Experiences in the Music business.

I wrote this book because I see so many Artists that are in the Music Industry that have not been properly educated on what is about to happen to them, how to handle Success, Failure and maintaining their Wealth.

INTRO

I was born in Biloxi, Mississippi. Willie Hugh Reese is my Father's name. I'm a Southern Boy.

My Dad and I moved from Gulfport Mississippi to Los Angeles California. My Life consists of playing Football and learning from my dad, where I learned about real struggle , strong discipline and hard work. I quickly found out what it takes to achieve any goals you set.

JAIL - My Artist name Dirty Rat was created in jail while I was serving my sentence. Honestly while I was in jail I got into a few fights, so I spent my last 6 months out of the 18-month sentence in what they called " The Hole " as a punishment. Funny, a few weeks later a rat came into my cell every night looking for food. I started feeding the rat by leaving my nasty jail food on the plate I didn't finish for the rat. Time went by & I started feeling like I was the rat in the hole. I felt so dirty, had no shower & when they fed us, they called it a " Mothball ". That was when the sheriff's took all the food on your plate and smashed it into one big football and then handed you warm milk with a smile. Living in horrible surroundings daily I named myself the " Dirty Rat " because no matter how dark, cold, scarry, hungry, funky I was & even with all those terrible situations I was in, I was still writing songs and focused on my career. I was writing new songs in my little dark hole. Bottom line is , I was still

Dedicated to my music no matter what.

When I was released from jail, I quickly became one of the best Battle Rappers on the Westcoast. I won awards on Radio Shows & many Rap Contest for Cash and Prizes.

Life with #34 Big Shaquille O'Neal - The main thing that I learned while being in Shaq's entourage was he taught me about money & the causes and effects of the Money. He also taught me that [Teamwork makes all the Dreams work] If all ur Folks can work together then all your folks can get Rich together !! It's as Simple as that.

The introduction of Cali Boi - The Song writer, The Producer and The Executive

When the Music Business changed in 2010, I quickly understood what I was then, and what I wasn't anymore because of my musical style & lyrics just wasn't the same as what was already playing nonstop on Radio Stations. My dad always said [A man has gotta know his limitations] Here's a quick Example (In 2022 Snoop Dog, Ice Cube, E-40 & Too Short) did an album together & it didn't sell a million copies but new artist like 21 Savage , Lil Baby & Da Baby sold 2 or 3 million album's each and that was a little puzzling to me. Funny because that's the same thing that happened in 2010 with some other new artist's that came out and were not very talented - selling millions of records while the true talented artists were getting no radio airplay and being pushed to the side. This has been going on for the last 15 years, so I became a songwriter & a music producer. I started Grinding in the music scene and a few years later because of my relationships I became a Music executive. I was employed by a few major Record Labels, so I believe my Credentials are adequate enough to write this book for the rookies and the veteran Artist.

So, enjoy this musical brain transplant - learning how to be Smarter and stay Successful in the Music Business.

GOOD LUCK & GOD BLESS

3

PREFACE

The music industry is a broad category that includes a variety of businesses and organizations involved in the production, distribution, and promotion of music. The industry includes record labels, music publishers, music venues, artist development and artists management companies, concert promoters and many more. The music industry is constantly evolving, and new technologies and business models have emerged in recent years.

The industry has been impacted by several challenges, including the rise of digital music, the decline of physical album sales and the consolidation of the major record labels. Despite these challenges, the music industry is still a large and thriving multi-billion-dollar business. Honestly you are about to enter one of the hardest industries to become successful in. Getting into the music business is harder than becoming a professional sports athlete. [I'll explain this later] 50% of the artists that are signed will probably get distributed to the world. The other 50% can simply become a Tax Right Off. 25% of the Artist that are signed just make enough money in their careers to live on and they'll have to budget that money probably their entire lifetime, But if you're one of the very few that actually do make it into the Music Industry with a good product this can become one of the most exciting and rewarding life changing events.

With that said, let's get right into -

THE 10 COMMANDMENTS

CHAPTER I

FAME IS GIVEN AND TALENT IS A GIFT AND SUCCESS IS A BLESSING.

CREATING YOUR BRAND

Many kids dream of becoming a movie star, a singer, or a Rapper. More evident now with the emergence of shows like American idol, the Voice, and countless other singing sites. The internet has made that dream more accessible and now Tik Tok and Snapchat artists are really emerging. But the old school rules remain the same. It may be easier to get your music to the general public, but the ultimate goal is to get a record deal from an accredited company. There are 5 important major record labels left because of countless mergers. Virgin Records, Capitol Records, Sony Records , Warner Brothers & Universal Music Group.

One of the most important thoughts about becoming an artist is being yourself and doing what you love. Make the music that makes you happy. To get the attention of these Record Labels you may assume that you need to make the music that interests the Public. In this business that's not necessarily so. What makes you unique is what's going to get your foot in the door.

Record labels are on a constant hunt for new artists. The artist is what keeps the record labels afloat. So much money goes into creating " the package." If the label does not view you as marketable, you will not get signed. It's sad to say but please realize your just numbers to all the Record Labels. 1st, it's your social security number, to get you paid. The 2nd and 3rd numbers are your driver's license and birth date so they could get you a car and know that you're legal to drive it, and also start up a bank account for you. 4th and 5th is How much money is the Artist going to need to do their album and How long will it take to make that money back to the Company. 6th, How much money are we going to make back after the Artist album goes public. They don't really care about your family issue's or whatever problems you may be facing in real life. They want you to turn the album in on the date and the deadline they set for you. Then more numbers, like the date you're putting the album out. So please don't get your feelings hurt in the formalities. They will sign you & give you a half of a million dollars to do an album, smile in your face and party with you, pop open some tasty Champagne bottles but at the end of the day they are in the business of making more number's and that's Money for the Company. You will never be the only number the label is dealing with. After your number is up another number begins in the form of a new artist.

Many people don't understand that the more unique you are with your craft, whether it's playing instrument's or using your voice as an instrument, the better your chances. Some artists are born gifted and very exceptional like Whitney Houston, Christina Aguilera, Michael Jackson. They were born with the gift of their voice. The other very talented artists have to develop their gifts. Many artists become who they are based on the music they grew up listening to. Very few people invent a new style, everything has been done before. Back in the day it was called biting or stealing, copying etc. Talent comes a dime a dozen, but if you have swagger aka personality, an image, uniqueness sets you apart from the rest. Your craft is your talent and that is what makes you special.

Developing your craft is just as important as having a craft. To become a Master of your craft you need to make an effort to practice it every day. Having the passion for your craft is just not enough. I learned it takes Effort plus Skills to equal Achievements. Educating yourself on your craft. What does it take to perfect your craft? It takes 10,000 hours to become a Master at whatever you want to be. Example - if you want to be a basketball player, you have to put in your 10,000 hours of grinding. That means from the playgrounds when you were little to playing from morning until dark, playing ball after school, playing in the park leagues and on the travel teams. Now you have countless days and nights as a high school player with all the practices and the Allstars leagues too. All those hours put in and combined and you still going to need at least 3 more years in your professional career to become a master. It's funny Kobe Bryant said " all this training I did when I was younger got me ready for this, but one day in his 2nd or 3rd year he said that's when it all clicked for him and made sense and now the game became easier and slower to him. He became The Black Mambo and you saw his greatness.

So what is your purpose? Why do you want to become an artist? Do you just want to get Rich? Do you want to be famous? What is your game plan? What type of music do you want to represent your style? How do you want to distribute or present your style? Do you want to go the route of obtaining an independent distribution deal or a major pop music deal? You can also go the nontraditional route being fully independent. Some labels want you to have your image and name already trademarked and copyrighted. I like to let most artists know to do the " Poor Man's Copyright " if you mail whatever it is, a song, logo, poem. Mail it to yourself and never open the envelope. This can protect you in most copyright infringement cases because the government stamped the sealed envelope with your information inside and it also has a date on it as well so you should win any court case.

Find out whatever your craft is and find an expert in your field to help you along the journey. Emulate your favorite artist. See what makes them so special. Maybe it's the singing runs they can do with their voice. Maybe you can do it better than them. Practice over the artist instrumentals, yes on their songs. You may think you can sound better than the original artist. Look at all the artist's first singles. That first song tells who they basically are. Research their managers, producers, their Record labels distribution to see why they signed the artist. Drinking hot tea before sleeping and after you wake up is super awesome because it will lubricate your throat. This will keep your money maker always oiled ready and healthy. Perform songs while you're workout, sing your songs on a treadmill or while moving. This will be a double double for you because you will build up super stamina and endurance, also keep you in shape for all your live performances. You will gain infinite breath while on the stage and be able to last the entire performance without getting tired.

If you want to be in this business, you will have to overcome stage fright and get out there on smaller stages like showcases and talent shows to overcome that fear. Perform in front of mirrors to see yourself and critique your facial expressions while performing. Remember the cameras will be right in your face during performances. Welcome positive & negative feedback by your peers, family and friends. Practice, Practice, Practice.

What type of artist are you? Are you a song writer Or Do you want to produce music? Songwriting and music producing are 2 different things. Songwriters write songs. If you're a producer
and you write songs too, that's how you make the most money.

This is the list of where all the money goes as following:

1] Record label
2] Attorney
3] Producers and Songwriters 4] Management
5] Taxes
6] The Artist
In that order.

If you're a songwriter, you need to register a cool name with a performing rights company [Publishing Company] (BMI, ASCAP, or SESAC), you're entitled to the writer's share of the royalty for a song, which is 50%. That other 50% goes to the publisher. If you're a songwriter and don't have a publisher, you're leaving that other 50% for someone else to grab off the table. When you start your own publishing company with one of the names I said above, then you can register your songs as the publisher as the performing rights company, then you'll receive the full 100% of royalties. Starting a publishing company is quick and easy just go online.

So much has changed in the record industry over the last few decades. Many artists are finding success by using social media and online streaming to promote and distribute their music. But if you are still going the traditional route, there are 5 major record labels left. During the Covid-19 outbreak from 2020 until present, Universal Music Group bought the majority of the independent record labels and put them all under the Universal Music Group's umbrella. Now they own 60% of the music industry.

CHAPTER II

PERCEPTION IS EVERYTHING, U CAN STILL BE BROKE BUT LOOK LIKE A MILLION DOLLARS.

BUILDING YOUR IMAGE

What do you feel like your image should be? Your image should be you showcasing you. What do you want to say to the world about your art? How do you want to present yourself? Some may build their image based on an artist that they admire the most. In the music business sometimes your image is more important than your artistry or quality of the music. One can argue that Lady Gaga's image for example the "Meat Suit" was more memorable than the song she sang. While her image was to shock you, her artistry will forever be undeniable. Your vocals, look, choice of costume or attire, album covers etc. should all be included to become the total package. Your vibe and style should both reflect what you want the world to know about you. If you're a party person and make party songs, no one really wants to hear you do a sad song. Always know who you really are. Funny fact: when I first met Micheal Jackson he never heard my music before but he loved my name Dirty Rat (my Brand) and he kept saying " Dirty Rat " for like an hour. "Omg I just love your name." Imagine his soft voice yelling out Dirty Rat and it was hilarious. He became my fan of my Brand and not my music. The point is - your look and your brand - are everything.

How do you present yourself? A lot can be said on how to act when you're trying to become an entertainer and aiming for a record deal. Just like employers may check out a candidate's social media to see if they are a correct fit to join the culture at work. Record labels also check out your social media pages to learn about their potential artist. The label can find out if you believe in yourself enough to promote your own art. What type of following do you have and how many followers do you really have? Whether you're difficult to work with. Remember someone is always watching. If you believe you're a superstar, act like one. But stay Humble.

You have to make a decision: do you want to be famous or popular? It's a big difference. Famous is like Eminem who has been out of the spotlight 4 many years. You won't see him walking around the neighborhood or at a Walmart trying to be seen. Do you want Popularity? Where you're looking to be seen everywhere and you crave all the cool attention. Do you just want to be rich? Do you want to be a songwriter or a music producer? Do you want to be a music engineer or
become a manager behind the scenes? Take your time and think about what's gonna feed your belly the best.

Your appearance. What type of style do you have? It is very important to pay attention to your hair, makeup, the clothes you wear, your vibe or energy. Everything says something about the artist that you are, so put your artistry together. Visualize who you are first. Write it down on a piece of paper & draw what you look like. It is a lot easier to visualize yourself if you write it down on a piece of paper.

What do you want your brand name to be or represent? Your logo (example are the many artists logos and brands) Take your time and pick something that has good eye candy. Something that someone would love to put on a t-shirt, a hat, books or a poster on their wall. Something that's creative that says you. Always think about marketing and branding yourself.

How will you get your music in front of people? First start with family and friends. Social media, podcasts, streaming sites. Do a lot of free shows. Right now you're not getting paid anyways to perform. Lawyers and doctors do pro-bono work so you should too. Also you never know who is in the audience to see someone else performing & then see you perform and BOOM!!! They like you too.

Start a Publishing Company before Recording your own music. The first thing I need you to do before recording any music is start a publishing company. It's a free service provided and there's many companies to choose from to help you. Honestly it's a very simple process.

Keep all your Publishing! Keep all your Publishing! Artist's songs have to be buzzing somewhere like the strip clubs, nite clubs on social media or on the radio before a record label spends a dime on your promotional tour's and music videos.

Remember all this money going out to your career needs to be put back in the pot from your album sales, publishing and royalties. Labels will provide tour support if the artist is selling songs. They will know exactly what artist to put on the tours and the different cities where their songs are selling. Think of a cool theme for your tours, make the name weird or very interesting or even a common name everyone can relate to or feel familiar " The Peanut Butter Tour " Believe me it works.

MONEY ADVANCES

The less money you take upfront from the record labels the more money you get in return from your album sales. If you believe in your craft, then take a smaller advance and keep grinding to keep the majority of the music gumbo. Now you can ask for a lot of money upfront but the Dark side of that is now you'll owe them the majority of your album sales. It's basically your decision on how well you think you will do when the world hears your music.Either you are all in or you're not.

Learn how to build your own professional studio. It may cost about $2000. Turn your bedroom, office or closet into a soundproof studio. Use Pro Tools as your software for the most professional sound. It's the standard software, 85% of engineers and studios use to lay your music. If you can save up $200.00 a month for one year, that's $2400 and now you have a studio. It's only one year later and the music game will not change and pass you by in one year. Listen, by doing this you are creating your own future if you just wait a year. Also you are saving money by not paying for outside studio time. Another plus is that your Masters or product will always be in your own computer where you will have full control over who gets to listen or utilize them. It's a microwave society so build your own studio.

You want to keep your own masters with you. Another advantage could be that you can now rent your studio out to other artists and make your money back by helping others to. You can become the spot that everyone spends $500 to do their demo's at. Before you have created your own studio or paid for studio time honestly I don't condone this, but I would take instrumental beats and songs off the internet to perfect my craft before recording any music. For obvious reasons I don't condone this behavior because if you tried to put it out you would be stealing. Copyright infringement.

Before you take your demo to a record label, I've learned that to be taken seriously you must present a professional looking E.P.K. [electronic press kit]. I also learned that every music executive will not listen to your music unless it was referred to them by someone in the entertainment business, or a person they know. Sometimes that's a positive and a negative 50/50. The music industry person that has the connections could be a client from the past and they did either good or bad business with them, but overall No One's gonna hear your music if it isn't brought in by an Industry person. You can google musical engineers & please don't be lazy, choose a good one.. I can tell if you don't take pride in how even and clean your music sounds so take your time and choose wisely.

CHAPTER III

*YOU'RE TOM BRADY AND EVERYONE ELSE HAS TO BE A TEAM PLAYER OR
THEY NEED TO BUILD THEIR OWN TEAM.*

BUILDING YOUR TEAM

Find a good lawyer you can trust. Not many layers can be trusted in the music industry because they all know each other, you know they go to the same gyms, sports bars etc. It's good to find someone outside the business that knows the business. You feel me? Attorney's run in the same circles and you can get caught up in attorney's relationships and that can hurt you when it's time to negotiate your contract. They may be dishonest and produce a favorable contract for themselves secretly and that will not be in your best interest. Finding a good manager - You don't need a manager in the beginning until you have something to manage. Don't waste time or money paying for a Manager to help you until you are established. Become your own manager and advocate for yourself. You pay your own bills, take care of yourself and kids plus you go to work, so they don't have anything to manage right now, unless they go get something else to manage to earn their percentage.

Finding a good producer is not easy but if you can find one that you click and vibe with that's awesome. If you don't vibe together, it's gonna be only about the money with him and sometimes you can hear it in the music. Get to know your producer and find out what music he likes to produce the most. Work with songwriters you can connect with. No egos just putting songs together and having fun. Let them get to know you so they can write a song that best fits you.

Bring in other artists around you that are as good or better than you. Because if you don't, you will not be challenged. If you're better than everyone in your click you will always believe you're the best. You will become stagnant and not grow. Be around someone that challenges you and makes you want to be better. I remember I was hanging out with Will Smith, Jamie Foxx, Brian McKnight and a couple more celebrities and we met at a spot in the parking lot. I saw about 3 million dollars in luxury pulling up and my Truck wasn't on their level. Honestly it made me think that I gotta step my game up if I'm gonna hang out with celebrities. I think It kept me focused. You should try it or at least go places celebrities go whenever possible(even if you have to save up to do it at least once every three months).

When you do need a manager: You need to have all this mapped out before you go get the record deal. Know who rode with you while you were broke and unsigned. But if you do acquire a manager, or other professional services here are some terms you need to know very well.

A Manager - is a professional in the industry who works closely with all aspects in the business to help an artist bring their goals to fruition. A manager works for you. A manager handles your external career affairs. He makes sure you get to your meetings, meet all your deadlines, he makes your important phone calls, makes sure you're at shows, books your hotel rooms and flights. A manager makes sure you're comfortable and happy. They work for you. I repeat they work for you. If you get paid, they get paid. He must put in the work for his percentage.

You don't have to sign a contract for a manager to manage your affairs. This could be a verbal agreement for you at that time. You don't have to commit to only one manager. The current manager can book a show for you and you make $5000, you give him his 20% [$1,000] and you [$4,000] Whereas if you sign with a manager he is your manager for the duration of the contract. The upside and downside are, if you do very well in the show and a more experienced manager approaches you with a better opportunity, you're stuck with that manager until the contract ends. The upside is when you have no contract ties with the current manager, so you can sign with a new manager. There is no loyalty in this Music Business. It's all about the business.

If the manager makes you sign to them, you are tied to them for however long your contract imposes. Choose wisely who you pick as your manager. Some managers may have many connections and know a few good producers and executives that can help or hurt you. It all depends if they do or did good or bad business with the companies in the past. So be picky and choose wisely.

A Producer - A music producer or record producer, assists artists and guides their songs bringing their passion and vision to life. The producer produces the music, song, beats and instruments. They listen to what you say and If they love it , it's a thumbs up but if they don't like it , well it's a thumbs down. They may help you write the song and produce a beat. He makes sure your song is mixed and mastered correctly that meets the industry standards and your vision. They also make sure the finished product is sent to the right people such as the manager and executives and gets it to the record labels. If you're a dope artist and a producer sees the value in working with you, you may not have to pay any money to be produced until after you start making some money. If you're an average artist you may have to pay for your studio time and I'm sorry for saying this but it's my experience. A good artist if the producer thinks you're that talented, they may not charge you for any studio time. I will invite you to the studio for nothing because I see the value in you. On some days when the producer you've been working with is tired and doesn't really want to come into the studio that day, they may still show up anyway because you guys have a great relationship. When you can laugh and create music together, that's priceless.

THE ENGINEER - MIX/MASTER-

A music engineer is a technical specialist. He controls the operations and the setup. This may include operating the equipment, recording edits and mixes. The engineer takes the product and makes it professionally sonically sound for the radio. He takes everything you do and enhances it ten times. They mix the songs to make sure everything is mixed evenly. The volume, the medium ranges, the highs, and lows. So no one has to adjust the volume while listening.

Music Attorney or Entertainment Attorney -

Is a specialized attorney that deals with legal issues surrounding the music industry. Basically contract management, copyright claims, artist representation, disputes and copyright claims. They negotiate all the deals, they will agree on your behalf. He makes sure your interests are legally protected.

HYPEMAN / CREW

Keep good friends around you that will ground you and tell you the truth. Positivity is the key. Have people in your circle that are not yes men or women. Backup dancers and singers, security, girlfriends, boyfriends. Secure who's going to support you in the beginning when you were not famous.

CHAPTER IV

PEOPLE GET ARROGANT HAVING 100,000 FOLLOWERS BUT THEY'LL NEVER MEET 100,000 PEOPLE IN THEIR REAL LIFE. DON'T GET CAUGHT UP IN THE FAKE FAME.

SOCIAL MEDIA FOLLOWING

"Back in the day" Record labels would discover a talent, they would pay for all related costs to get their artist in front of an audience. You would take a meeting, sing in front of the executives of the record label. The record label would sign the artist and develop a team. Give you upfront money. Pay for your singing lessons, image consultants, marketing, and promotional tours. They would upfront the total cost to develop your Image and direct your career. Many record labels lost so much money doing it this way. Some labels after signing you and getting you into the studio and finding out that you're mediocre at best and not that talented after spending big budget money on vocal coaches, marketing and producers. The label would spend $500,000 more than another 2,000,000 to put your album out. Just for the album not to do well. So much spent and so much lost just to acquire you as their artist.

Today, labels want to see a real generous amount of support from the public, family or friends. Record labels want to know that you have a significant number of followers. There are many ways for them to research information to see if your following is legit and not fake followers that you might have purchased. They want to see likes as well as dislikes. You have 100,000 likes but not 1 dislike? Red flag. It's always going to be someone that dislikes your music - everywhere.

Also, people are paying over $1000 for 1 million followers and most of the profiles have one post or no profile pictures; they're newly created. Although having a huge following does not necessarily mean that you will or will not get a record deal, it may show the label that your music was not good enough to warrant a huge following or you did not promote yourself enough.

Use social media as a gauge to promote yourself to family and friends. There are several factors that a label would consider, like album or EP sales, press coverage, touring, play count and how much you are in demand. But let's keep it real, sometimes you can just be a friend or family member of a record executive and get a record deal, but that still doesn't mean you will become a star.

Today you need to have a fanbase. Before they would spend one cent on you, they need to know that you will make them money. Your own fan base increases the chances that they will support your music and concert sales. Social media is a small part of obtaining a record contract. You will also need a (EPK) electronic press kit which is really a video resume (an artist statement, show your manager, the performances under your belt, EP's already recorded and mastered and mixed. Then again if we really like an artist, and we see the value and believe that we are going to make money off of you, your social media following will not matter.

If the label likes you, they will all listen to it and if they think your record is good then they will call you in for a meeting to perform for the executives. The label discusses, how did they look? How did they perform? What do we think he's going to bring to the table? Is he a gold, platinum, or a multi-platinum potential artist? That lets us know how much of a budget that we will allocate for that artist and in what location or state, because the label knows down to the city what they like and will spend money on. Like which city's like country or pop or r & b. The label checks in with the radio stations and see's what type of music is being played mostly in that area. Basically so they can gauge what markets to hit like Hip Hop, K-pop, R&B and Latin hip-hop.

Many people don't know but record labels have to listen or deal with at least 100,000 artists every month which is 1,200,000 artists a year. Jazz Rock, pop, hip hop, country, R&B and K-pop to figure out who's good or not. Everyone wants to be famous. It's harder to make it in the music industry than to become a professional sports athlete. Professional sports have at least 7 rounds of draft picks each year. So 30 teams pick five athletes in a five round draft, so that's 150 new athletes getting a real chance to show their gifts on the field. The music labels each only put out about 10 new artists a year. Take 5 labels, that's only 50 new artists.

This info can be discouraging, but it is not impossible. If you think about it, how many new artists do you really hear on the radio per year? Of those new artists even the radio stations pick and choose who they will rally behind and give them air time on the major radio broadcast channels. They tell all the radio stations to play what music and what artist.

CHAPTER V

YOU'LL FIND THAT THE GRIND TAKES TIME FOR THE MIND TO CATCH THE SIGNS SO TALENT CAN SHINE.

INVESTORS & ACCOUNTANTS –

Find people that have the money that don't need the money back now. Period. People that need the money back now will hound you nonstop for the money back long before you are able to realistically give it - they'll make you want to pull all your hair out and theirs.

If you find an investor that doesn't need the money back right away (pray, pray, pray) and he believes in your talent, those investors understand how long it will potentially take to make their money back. Don't get a criminal investor. They will get their money back and now he is expecting to tie you in for life with him. He'll say " My Money made you " You will forever owe him even after the money is paid back in full and with some interest. Don't do it.

Always have a contract when you're dealing with investors. Get your money up front. Yes upfront. They are just investors, not your boss. Many investors feel if they loan you the money, they can tell you what to do with it and your career. Aim for getting all the money you are borrowing upfront.

Accountant

What's a good CPA? That's a difficult question to answer. I guess if they are not broke that's a start. Seriously you should ask any independent, mainstream artists that you might know, who they deal with and who do they trust. You have to start there with family, friends and those associates because you never know they might have met. It could be someone at church that's perfect for you and your career.

Background check that person because remember they're dealing with your money and you don't want to be another story about an artist not paying taxes or going broke from overspending. You got to much money going out and not enough money coming in.

Find a parent or relative with business knowledge, maybe a friend or family member that recommends an accountant because you need to trust the person that manages your money and Taxes. Many wealthy people have fallen because of the untrustworthy accountant. You have to trust that person. They also deal with your taxes. Many celebrities have lost work or fallen to faulty taxes or not paying taxes.. In 1990 Willie Nelson was hit with a $32,000,000 bill for back taxes. Look what happened to Lauryn Hill. Lauryn spent 3 months in jail in 2012 for failing to pay over 1,000,000 in back taxes. There are many sad countless stores like this so please take care; it is very important.

Try not to borrow money from family and friends. They will harass you for the money back. Maybe even before you have made 1 cent from the record labels. You will need to focus on the project and not worry about paying them back.

CHAPTER VI

CONTRACTS ARE LIKE BAD GIRLFRIENDS, YOU CAN GET OUT THE RELATIONSHIPS BUT IT WON'T BE EASY.

TEACHING YOU CONTRACTS

Most contracts given to the artist, when the label wants to sign you, are standard contracts that you can find a dime a dozen on the internet. Surprisingly, most artists do not give it the attention it deserves. The under 20 page document contains your name, social, and other personal information on the first page. On the contract you will find how many albums we require of you. Any money that we will or already have advanced to you, your budget. This is by design. The label wants you to go " OMG". Labels want you to become so excited seeing all the possibilities. The labels will always ask you to look the contract over with a lawyer and get back to them asap.

If you can't come prepared with a lawyer, get one as soon as possible to look over your contracts. Many artists use a parent or family member that they feel is knowledgeable to look over their contract. The contract looks enticing to them too and they are enticed by the numbers also. They will encourage and give you the ok to sign the contract, even without a lawyer ever looking it over to see if this is in your best interest or not. Big Mistake ! The fallout from that is when you approach the label for an advance when record sales have risen and your label asks you " did you look at your contract? The contract states you don't make money until this happens or this money is paid back totally. Pay the money, attain a lawyer. Your contracts are very vital to your career. It can and will make or break you.

Look at the group TLC. TLC made $30,000,000; they were supposed to split $10,000,000 each. However, after paying the record label, the team, the entourage etc. & the dust was cleared, the 3 person group only pocketed about $2,000,000 each before their taxes. Read your contracts. Not only read your contracts, negotiate the best deals for you or have an attorney on deck to negotiate the best terms.

How to get out of a bad contract. Here is a gem I'm spilling. You want to get out of a bad contract? Ok say you blow up and you become this big mega star on your first album. You sell 2,000,000 records at $10.00 a piece. That's $20,000,000. You get 10% of that which is $2,000,000 before taxes. The label may offer you $500,000 for an advance to do your next album. It's in your contract to do another album with them. Knowing that you're in a messed up contract that you signed there's no other way around the pay that you already received. But if you are trying to negotiate a future advance? This is where you have the power. Based on your previous album sales you can go to the label and negotiate for a bigger advance. This is how you wiggle out the contract by realizing that your record sales were $20,000,000 and the label takes their portion. You get what was legally stated in the contract. You want more of the pot? Then you must ask for a bigger advance. Now remember the advance is supposed to be spent on making your next album. I told you I was going to discuss how to get out of a bad contract.

The only way to get out of your contract is to refuse to do another album. Retire! That's right kick it on an island like every day is summer or on your coach but kick it. Then the label will have to try to renegotiate. You signed for like 4 albums. If you made a lot of money for the label the label may negotiate with you to give you more money. It's a risky move. You have to gamble that you are worth it to the label. That the label will tear up the contract and produce a whole new contract. You can stipulate a $2,000,000 advance to do your next album. That might be all you would have made anyway after your album sales. There's a chance your second album won't hit that amount in money due to you. But at least you have the money upfront whether the album does well or not.

Even if you are new to the business and just starting out you will certainly need a lawyer. Pick a lawyer you can trust. Do your research. When you're an entertainment lawyer, they run in a lot of the same circles. Consult with other artists as to their experience with that lawyer. Lawyers can help with disputes with copyright infringement, trademark issues etc. Many artists are so excited to get the deal and receive a substantial amount of money they ignore the terms of the contracts.

Always negotiate the deal.

Depending on your location you will be flown in to meet the executives. There is a process, let's go through the levels. An A & R person will schedule a meeting where you would meet the mid-level executives, then another meeting is scheduled if you make it where you would meet with the higher level executives at the label. Everybody on all levels has to agree on your songs, album or product. When the product comes from the A & R They'll take the product to the streets where your song will be distributed to the clubs, barber shops, radio station DJ's, strip clubs. Those are the people we trust to give us unbiased feedback. After everyone listens to the product. You may be scheduled for another meeting where feedback is presented from the streets, A & R executives and maybe a few DJ's. The last meeting is with the V. P.'s and the president's of the company. They will decide Yay or Nay whether your product has made it through the process.

Remember, if the Record label really likes you, they will retain you. They will not let you leave without signing a contract or at least close to signing it. So consider yourself blessed. They see value in you as an artist and they feel they will make a lot of money by getting you to sign with their label.

On the flip-side, Record labels have been known to retain you just to keep you from signing with other labels. Depending on the contract you sign, they can legally prevent you from legally doing a record deal with any other label for a stated amount of time, whether they use your music or product and release it for airtime. Essentially you can be shelved, that means the label can write you off on their taxes and leave you without ever putting out 1 single.

If you sign, they own your name, your image, your likeness they call now (N I L). Which means everything you make under the umbrella of your artist name, the label will own a piece of it for the stipulated amount of time on the contract. So please read your contracts. Make sure that this is the label that you want to be committed to.

CHAPTER VII

*ALWAYS REMEMBER WHERE YOU STARTED FROM BECAUSE WHERE YOU
END UP JUST MIGHT NOT BE WHERE YOU WANTED TO GO.*

AFTER YOU SIGN A RECORD DEAL

Once you sign, you will be appointed a team as mentioned in Chapter 3 but, in addition, an image consultant, social media consultant, agent/booking agent and a publicist - Here are several more term you need to know like your first and last name.

An image consultant is a person that is hired to give you advice about ways to improve your public image. This person also makes sure your wardrobe, hair and image is properly representing your brand.

Social Media Consultant's are agencies or individuals who work with their clients to optimize their social media presence.

Booking agent. Music agents work with artists to schedule concerts, tours, interviews, and to negotiate contracts and fees for bookings like club performances.

Publicist. Also called a press agent, public relations counselor generates media attention and manages public relations for musical artists and music related businesses.

Be prepared when you are signed to a label & expect everything to move very fast. Be flexible. When I signed to LOUD Records Steve Rifkind was the CEO, I had one meeting with the executives, street team, marketing team and media design team. I worked on my 6 song demo for like 9 months and it was funny when Rifkind played the first song and stopped it before it finished. He looked at me with a grin and said " congratulations and welcome to LOUD Records. It can happen that simple and fast. Within two weeks I received my cash advance and a booked flight to NYC to meet the executives there. You will get very little sleep, you will also be traveling, meeting other label mate's and executives, producers, It will become a whirlwind of goodness. Take note : The label owns you now.

Don't be surprised if they want you to sit down for six months like they did me and made me wait a year behind Wu-Tang Clan and Big Pun after I signed. But I truly believe that I needed that world touring experience doing real big shows. They can shut you down if they want. Or at least your name down. You have no recourse, you signed on the dotted line. So if someone asks you to perform in China they may pay you $1,000,000 to perform. If you decide to do the show without the record label's knowledge The record label can sue you. They own your brand name and likeness. So you have to pay attention to your contracts. I cannot stress that enough.

Don't be blinded about the money you receive upfront; it's your entire future career that's on the line. When I was' ' Dirty Rat " the rapper, Shug Knight offered me $1,000,000 to sign to Death Row Records. Shug was notorious for how he treated the artists that were signed to his label. It was not favorable. So as attractive as the amount he offered me to sign, I couldn't take the money. Nobody wanted to support Mr Knight. If I would have signed to Death Row Records. He would have owned my name, brand and likeness. I would have had a $1,000,000 advance to do my album for him. I would've spent $500,000 on making my album awesome and have $500,000 in my pocket. See the problem is nobody would have supported my music or put it on the radio and no DJs were going to play it in the clubs because at that time many people thought Death Row was shady and Mr knight had Tupac Killed. This was after Snoop Dog and Dr Dre left. Shug was trying to rebuild the label after his big name artist left. A

28

Death Row contract back then was considered a " Death Contract " very few wanted to work with Mr Knight. I knew that if I would have taken his money based on how Shug spoke to his artist and hit on his artist that we would have problems. If he would've hit me I would've hit him back and I don't think my outcome would've been good for me. He still had a lot of Power back then. All money is not good money. Always be careful. I had to respectfully turn Mr Knight down.

Now back to your team. You have the full team. You have at least 6 people along with the record label aka " The Machine " that believe in you and are working to help you become successful. Now you are unitedly structured to take over the world. Now go take over the world. But bear in your mind that Everything has its moments and time pattern. It's sometimes the timing. You can come out with a great album, if it's not the right time for it it won't sell. For example you can be an awesome artist and plan to drop your buzzing single in November. The Major labels generally drop the Major artist during the holidays. Usually the last 3 months of the year. Around Halloween for the Christmas Season. If you put out your album in November but the major artists like Drake, Da Baby, Beyonce and Taylor Swift all have albums that are dropping at the same time as you are dropping, you may be overlooked. You can have a great album & a few hot singles but those things may not matter, because 80% of the major artist albums will come out with yours and they are going to be the public's first choice. Your album could be lost in the holiday sauce. The Public will listen to all the major artist's albums 1st for weeks before they listen to yours. It's all about the Timing.

How to cause a buzz with your music? If you can get yourself featured on an established artist album or song with millions of fans by doing a collaboration with them. That's when 2 or more artists do a project or song together and they split the publishing rights. Drop your album at the same time they are dropping their music. This technique gives you a boost to compete with major artists at the same time. Example, if you do a great collaboration with Drake and he's coming out at a certain date, it makes sense to drop your music in that period also. We don't know for sure what our future will be but if you do certain things while you're in the present we can definitely determine your future by your present actions. Everything happens for a reason.

Next, Fake it to make it; you can look like you're never Broke everywhere you go & don't make it easy to be contacted [accessible]. Many artists once they sign a deal they get some money, that is called a contract advance. Right away artists will spend it on jewelry, new cars, drugs, traveling and housing when they are supposed to be recording their album.

When the artist runs out of money, they want to ask for another advance of money, the label says no way jose but you can sell some of your publishing. We will convince you to sell 50% of your publishing. Not a good idea at all !! Labels may give you an advance of $50,000 or more for 50% of your publishing rights because someone at the label has done their research on you and determines the artist's value. They figure they will make at least $500,000 off your album so the advance is approved.

Now the artist is back to spending more money etc... Now the artist sells about $500,000 albums. That's $5,000,000 profit. Then the artists ask when am I going to get a portion of those sales? What artists don't realize is that the label now owns half of your publishing rights and spent $2,500,000 to put you out as an artist across the world, so the Label has to double that investment in you. So now you're in debt for about $5,000,000 that you have to pay back first. A gold album sale is $500,000 & you need to sell more than 500,000 gold to get $10,000 from the label. You need to sell more than gold to get at least $10,000.

Usually, you see a lot of artists upset wondering where the money is and complaining to social media because the artist hasn't received any additional money. Artists soon forget that if the Label spent $2,500,000 on an artist which includes all those cash advances paid to you and to do your album, you got to double their money back. Then when you exceed the $5,000,000 profit, then you get paid at least $10,000. See you only have 200% to work with on each album. Ok? 100% publishing & the other 100% album sales. Record Labels usually take 60% of album sales and if you sold any publishing, they get 50% of that also. Let's do the math, so you got 90% left .... 20% goes to your Taxes, and 25% goes to your producer's. 10% goes to Management. 10% goes to any co-writers & musicians.25% goes to you. The artist. So always Keep Your Publishing Rights. And use your money wisely. That is what's left of it. And avoid the family lending trap.

LOANING MONEY

Try not to loan family money. They will not pay you back. They will feel you don't need it back right away or at all. When you loan family money in your mind, give it as a gift. Don't tell them that, but know in your mind you may not ever get the money back so don't stress out about it. It's not worth losing a family member of money.

Making the Video making a video in the 1990's would cost the record label anywhere from $100,000 to $500,000. TLC spent like $3,000,000 on their music video Waterfalls. Where they basically used a green screen with water sprayers, a few fans blowing & props to stand up on while singing. They were not standing in a real waterfall at all. Mr Chris Robinson spent like $3,000,000 to do a 6 min music video whereas in many movies back then the whole budget was $3,000,000 to shoot a motion picture. Today Superstar Beyoncé recorded one of her latest music videos using 5 iPhone 12's . The new iPhones have 4 lenses so you can easily shoot music videos nowadays because everyone owns a smartphone with a camera.

The labels realized that you don't have to spend a lot these days to shoot a music video. No artist wants to think " what if my single, album or product doesn't do well. How come No One's buying my single anymore. Keep your head up even if you start thinking why, just refocus on the task because you can do it. If You have signed a 4-year contract with the label which does not guarantee a successful career. But you have signed a contract with the label that advanced you a sum of money. Depending on your contract you are guaranteed an increase every year that you have signed. If you were advanced $50,000 this year you may get $65,000 the next year. Negotiate your amount. Or the Record label can opt out but have to honor 2 out of the 4 years on your contract and then release you from that contract.

CHAPTER VIII

RELATIONSHIPS WILL BUILD YOU UP OR BREAK YOU DOWN, BUT EITHER WAY YOU NEED RELATIONSHIPS TO MAKE IT.

BUILDING RELATIONSHIPS

Don't burn up the bridges. The music industry is a very small but very POWERFUL industry. Be careful on how you handle all your relationships. You can have beef with just 2 people, go to another state and plan to do a big business deal and those same 2 people you could now care less about or don't even remember may be the 2 people who now stop you in your tracks. See you never know who knows who in this Industry. Your beef or reputation has preceded you and now your potential gig or deal fell through badly because you burned or pissed someone off or someone's friend, colleague, relative or associate that lives in that state. Here's a good case in point, Wesley Snipes who was at the top of his movie game until he had beef with a few people in the movie industry and was black balled. For over 10 years he couldn't get a big movie deal. You can mess over a manager and not think anything of it. Then you get a gig somewhere with another artist, maybe a big collab you've been waiting on that could be game changer. Then you come to seal the deal and get into the studio with this artist and you find out that his manager is the manager that you messed over. Ouch.

Now the deal either falls through like quicksand or now they are going to charge you dollars on top of dollars on top of dollars to record with his artist. Needless to say, you won't make it without relationships. You need somebody that knows somebody that knows somebody.

Endorsements come from relationships built with companies. If a company or brand likes or feels it's good business to partner with you because of your brand, they will ask you to represent their brand. You become the face or image of that company. Likewise your name and image becomes associated with the company and that company's products.

To build relationships you have to understand what relationships mean. You have to relate to riding in the ship together. If you don't relate you can't ride the ship together. Your relationships could sink you or keep you afloat. You need to relate to the people you are building industry relationships with. Understand the person you are dealing with. Are they about the money only? Do they have your best interest in mind or just theirs? I like to keep my industry relationships as associates.

Your family and friends can also just be your associates. Understand your relationships and how they work. Who are the true family and friends that care about your well being and checked on you before you signed your contract? You have people that keep you positive and exude positive energy, You have people that hate on you. You need all the above. The people that hate on you will motivate you to get better. The people on your team are depending on you to make it happen and to get paid to. The people that believe in you with the money are expecting you to double their investment.

When it comes to your team make sure that everyone on your team knows that there is only 1 Batman. Everyone else is Robin. You are the Boss. If your team doesn't understand that then they don't need to be on your team. Tell them to go make up their own team. When I worked with #34 Shaquille O'Neal, he often told the story about himself and Kobe Bryant [RIP] when they both played for the Lakers. Shaq was frustrated that Kobe was not passing the ball to the open player in the plays. He told Kobe `` Man this is a Team Sport and there is no "I" in the word Team. Kobe replied " but there's a M and an E " in it [ME] in there. Kobe was funny but you have to pay attention to how you treat your teammates, peers and relationships. When I was a part of Shaq's entourage, he paid us all the same pay so there would not be any animosity in the team. Mr Tom Brady can't throw the ball to himself. He needs the coach to tell him what to do. He needs the wide receivers to catch the ball. He needs the linemen to protect him from the players that are trying to tackle him. He needs the running backs to be sharp, possibly run and catch the football. Everybody's working as a team. The team understands their positions and roles. We need our team to be very successful. We also need them to acquire coveted endorsements.

Remember, Endorsements come from relationships built with companies. If a company or brand likes or feels it's good business to partner with you because of your brand, they will ask you to represent their brand. You become the face or image of that company. Likewise your name and image becomes associated with the company and that company's products.

Funny Fact: Back in the days, rappers would write bad songs about MC Hammer disrespecting him because in the 90's he did a Taco Bell commercial. He got paid one million dollars to do that and all the Rappers were upset calling him a sell out, he crossed over, homosexual and white washed. Crazy because today's Rappers would kill to be in a Taco Bell commercial and only get paid $50,000 and be seriously happy with it. Trust me I've done the deals for them.

It's a good idea if you can write some jingles for different products. I've done a few Hershey commercials, Reese's cups and some others. Finding a sponsor is not that easy but it's common to find one that will support your product while you're supporting their business. Sometimes you may not get any money upfront when you first go into business but eventually the money will come as the product's buzz spreads.

It's beneficial to you to keep your relationships with other artists in the business as successful or more successful than you are. If you want to collaborate with that artist, most artists want you to pay them. But if you have a relationship with that artist you could be collaborating for free. A lot depends on that relationship you have with that artist or any of the team members that have that artist's ear. " Method man came all the way from a club in L.A. to the 'Valley' that is San Fernando Valley at 2:00 am to record his rap verse for me on a track for free. That's because I had a great relationship with him & Wu-Tang Clan. He would never do that for any other artist without getting paid first unless he

34

had a good relationship with them.

The music business is all about relationships. Many of the projects that I have worked on in the past were brought about because of the relationships that I have built up my whole career.

♪

CHAPTER IX

IF YOU WERE ON YOUR DEATH BED, YOU WILL REGRET NOT EVER TRYING TO MAKE IT UNTIL YOU FAILED, AT LEAST YOU KNOW YOU TRIED.

DON'T EVER GIVE UP

There are people in the music industry that will discourage you. You're not getting work fast enough. You're not getting as much money as you are worth, or that goal is too hard for you to achieve. If they are in the music industry, they may have tried many things also and did not succeed. They will try to discourage you because they didn't make it themselves.

There was a homeless man who played the guitar in front of a popular convenience store by the LAX airport. One day a known artist got out of his Truck and started singing & playing his guitar with the homeless guy. They started vibing and playing a couple of known songs. After they finished singing, the artist was leaving and before he left he dropped a $100 bill into the man's offering plate. The 57 year old homeless guy said " hey wait " and handed the artist a manilla folder with an old dirty rubber band around it and said it was full of old songs he wrote his whole life. The artist left with the song's.

Over 8 months later the artist returned to that same store where he met the guy. One of the songs the homeless guy gave him he used and it went number one on the charts. Wow! The artist came back trying to locate the guy for month's. He finally found him and put him up in a condo, paid his bills, set him up with a publishing company to receive checks and gave him a bag of money basically, told him "congratulations man you wrote a hit song for a huge major recording rock group ". The songwriter never gave up, he may have slowed down because of certain circumstances but he did not quit.

Most people give up, that's why they tell you it's way too hard to accomplish. My dad always told me to look at that glass. He'd ask what do you see? I said " it's half empty right ? " But he said the glass is also half full, right? There's always 2 sides of thing's son.

Many people tried to discourage me from playing football, rapping, producing etc. If you have dreams and goals, whatever your dreams and goals are, don't let anyone discourage you from pursuing them. I found out that it is important to sometimes reinvent yourself with another name. I went from "Dirty Rat " the Westcoast lyrics to now " Cali Boi " the songwriter, music producer and executive. My friend 2 Chainz was originally Titti Boy like over 10 years ago before everyone knew him. Now he changed his name to " 2 Chainz " Sometimes it can take you years of grinding in the music underground scene before you finally become popular, but I'll say it again you have to be humble when you finally do because It can all leave in an instant. God don't like ugly and if you act ugly you will lose it all real ugly.

I've also learned if Doesn't really matter what name u pick, hey honestly think about it , you could be named " Baby CoCo Pig Dookie " and if you're music touches the heart and soul of humanity you will win and never lose your fan base. They'll always remember your first album and appreciate the way you made them feel when they first heard your song. That is priceless and they'll love that you're still out there Grinding on stages and coming to support you.

The Flip-side: Yes you knew it was coming. Sometimes If you have been out for a certain amount of years and you feel like you have done all you can do with your brand, sometimes it's best for you to adapt to what's current but keep your true self inside the music and change your name or style or look. My buddies " Tha Alcoholics " changed their name to " Tha Liks " and they're still world touring today. Snoop Dog changes his name frequently 1st it was Snoop Doggy Dog, then it was Big Snoop Dog, remember Snoop Lion the Jamaican? But know it's basically back to Snoop Dog but u get the point. Funny a lot of artists use their alias to seem younger or attack a different audience. I don't condone this behavior but you never know, it's like a baseball game when you're up to bat and you swing at a pitch, you never know it might be a Home run.

NEVER GIVE UP !!

You will experience many No's. If you believe in your craft, the No's make you go a lot harder and re-examine every aspect of your craft and make it better by taking and asking for criticism.

Always grow your skills to the highest level you can go to. Check your pride at the front door. There should be no gig that is beneath you. I have seen at least 5 artists get a record deal at a Free gig or small show because of perfect timing. The stars aligned when they showed up - they didn't know an A&R person was actually looking for some new talents and they saw their performance. And, BAM. There life changed Remember, this could happen to you. You are not a superstar yet, it's only in your mind right now. But it's coming. So please stay Humble.

CHAPTER X

*MONEY DOESN'T MAKE YOU RICH, IT'S WHAT YOU DO WITH ALL THE
MONEY MAKES YOU WHO YOU ARE.*

MAINTAINING THE SUCCESS 🍍 🍍 🍍

Once you have a hit record under your belt, you will certainly be sought out by many in the industry for future endeavors. Be very gracious. Because the music business's love doesn't last long, basically it's until your next record comes out and hopefully it's another hit song. You're only as good as your last hit. Hit records last 6-9 months on the radio. After your song loses the attention of the public, meaning as soon as it dies down, you have to turn in your next single to the record label. What if they don't like it? Now you've just become a one hit wonder by accident. It's not your fault it could be just the timing. Your first record was a hit but your second record bombed. You may lose many fans on your second album if it's a dud. Your fans can and will start second guessing you if you really were a good artist in the first place.

It's hard to make 2 songs that are hits. Most of the time the second record is never as good as the first record, so try to focus on starting out with 2 songs and music videos at the same time. So you can have a single and a follow up buzzing. Facts: Remember if you only get one hit song, you're very lucky and blessed. There are many artists that don't ever get a song on the radio or ever get a song that becomes really successful. Look at my buddy ' Tone Loc '. He had 2 hit songs " Funky Cold Medina " and " Wild Thing ". For 35 years he has been touring based on his only two hit singles. Always be humble and perform that song for everyone because remember that song you did is a success around the world, so you have to perform that song for people all around the world and that can take you a lifetime to do and have fun.

The first song you come out with is basically your true identity to the world. It's who they really are. " Too Short's first song was " Life is Too Short' Eazy E's first song was " we want eazy ". Remember how you sounded when you came out? That's your fan base. If you try to change and adapt to another sound, you may lose your fan base trying to gain a new market or age group. Very few have been able to change to a different genre of music without recourse. If you stay loyal to your fans they will stay loyal to you and continue to support you - forever. For example, you sell a million records being yourself and now you start to use auto tune on your vocals and it changes your sound. Now you have lost some of your fans. If you stay true to who you are, those fans will rock with you for life. My good friends Michael Jackson, DMX, GURU, Big Pun, Coolio, Nate Dogg, Whitney Houston are all gone, but their music will live forever. Only you can control your legacy so make sure you leave an imprint and have something to leave your family from your Legacy. Live to build your Legacy.

GOD BLESS

BONUS TAKE AWAYS:

There are many artists that pursue the fully independent route without a label or many followers on social media and no tracks ever recorded. Sometimes getting signed to a record label is not the only option. Many artists have become very successful by making their own contacts and building a reputation on their own without the aid of the huge Label network.

Become business savvy. Yes, when you're not getting as many gigs, the phone stops ringing and the money dries up. It may be a good idea to learn the business side of the music industry. There are so many different aspects of this business that do not require you to be the front person. Do your research, there must be something in this industry that interests you enough where you feel you can do it with your eyes closed.

My advice is do your research. It's not all glamorous. If you don't have the stomach for the music industry, join another profession and stay away from this pitfall of dreams and opportunities. But if you still want to join the community, always remember that you have the power and don't let anyone take it from you.

LASTLY, the most important thing I've learned from the music business is NO ONE Is your friend and loyalty is nonexistent. When it comes to the music business, your Integrity is not as important as your reputation. Yes I'll explain, your reputation is everything in this business and your integrity is only about 50% because everyone is a Savage in this Music Business, arrogant, heartless and pretty much thinks they should be entitled to everything and especially all the Superstar artists. I'm not being mean - just stating the facts from my experiences.

YOU CAN DO IT !!!! GOOD LUCK !

Made in the USA
Columbia, SC
05 November 2022